A LITERARY EXCURSION

TO THE

INNS OF COURT IN LONDON

DESCRIBED AND ILLUSTRATED

BY

TIMOTHY DANIELL

WILDY & SONS LTD
LONDON
1971

Wildy & Sons Ltd.,
Lincoln's Inn Archway,
Carey Street,
London, W.C.2A 2JD.

First published 1971
2nd Impression 1981
3rd Impression 1985

© 1971 Timothy Daniell

Front cover, Temple Bar, reproduced by kind permission of Rawlings & Sons Ltd.

I SBN 84490-001

Reprinted by
Hobbs the Printers of Southampton

To the memory of

LORD GODDARD

in gratitude

J.S.

... I have formerly lived
  by hearsay and faith,
   but now I go
   where I shall live
    by sight,
    and shall be
     with Him
  in whose company
 I delight myself . . .

Mr. Standfast, Pilgrim's Progress, pt. ii.
John Bunyan (1628-1688)

FOREWORD

Starting at the Bar now is very different to what it was. Called to the Bar in 1899, I accepted my first brief in the reign of our Sovereign Queen Victoria. In those days there was no scheme of Legal Aid to which everybody can now turn. Half a century later, in 1948, the Legal Aid Act was introduced. How far that has been an advantage to the Bar may be doubted.

    I have read this book. Mr. Daniell is to be congratulated in showing the uninformed layman what the Inns of Court represent in history and in the present day.

Easter 1971

THE RT. HON. LORD GODDARD, G.C.B.,
Lord Chief Justice of England 1946-1958.
Bencher of the Inner Temple.

ACKNOWLEDGEMENTS

This book is intended for such and every visitor to the Inns of Court, come he by chance or design. Having come he must see and he must wander. This framework, a companion of facts and anecdotes, is designed to assist that wandering.

This is not an official publication—God forbid! The thoughts and opinions offered in the pages ahead are as unofficial as is my responsibility for them. This book is not an authority. Those who need fill their thoughts with the scholars are recommended to other works: *Pereant qui ante nos nostra dixerunt*—may those perish who have said our good things before us.

It is an honour to mention my appreciations:
MR. O. TERRY, Under-Treasurer of Gray's Inn; CAPT. J. B. MORRISON, R.N., Under-Treasurer of the Middle Temple; LT.COL. BRIDGES, Under-Treasurer of Lincoln's Inn; and especially CMDR. FLYNN, Sub-Treasurer of the Inner Temple, who has been a light-house in troubled waters; MR. JACK EDWARDS, Librarian of Cheshunt; to the respective Librarians of the Inns and especially MR. P. C. BEDDINGHAM for untying quite a few of my knots; MR. ALAN MONTAGUE for valuable help; MR. JAMES HARKESS; MR. THOMAS ASPELL; my sister BELINDA for her toil; MR. GEORGE EDINGER, who lived in the Temple and survived the Blitz years there; my cousin HEATHER CHILD; MR. KEN SINKINS and WILDY'S for their able co-operation throughout; to the printers (whose only 'error' may have been to print this work).

Lastly, thanks be to those whose help will remain my simple secret, *gratia pro rebus merito debetur inemptio*—thanks are worthily due for things unbought. They and the reader encourage this pen.

T.D.
Gray's Inn, Easter Day, 1971

CONTENTS

LAWYERS IN ENGLAND
THOROUGHFARES: THE STRAND (ROYAL COURTS OF JUSTICE)
                           FLEET STREET
                           CHANCERY LANE

THE TEMPLE
TEMPLE CHURCH
MIDDLE TEMPLE: INTRODUCTION
                      THE LAMB
                      MIDDLE TEMPLE LANE
                      BRICK AND ESSEX COURT
                      NEW COURT
                      GARDEN COURT
                      MIDDLE TEMPLE GARDENS
                      QUEEN ELIZABETH BUILDINGS
                      FOUNTAIN COURT
                      MIDDLE TEMPLE HALL
                      PUMP COURT
                      THE CLOISTERS

INNER TEMPLE: INTRODUCTION
                    THE PEGASUS
                    INNER TEMPLE LANE
                    HARE COURT
                    MASTER'S HOUSE
                    INNER TEMPLE HALL
                    CROWN OFFICE ROW
                    INNER TEMPLE GARDENS
                    PAPER BUILDINGS
                    HARCOURT AND TEMPLE GARDENS
                        BUILDINGS
                    KING'S BENCH WALK
                    MITRE COURT BUILDINGS

LINCOLN'S INN: INTRODUCTION
                    THE ARMS
                    CAREY STREET ARCH
                    NEW SQUARE
                    OLD HALL
                    CHAPEL
                    OLD BUILDINGS
                    GATE HOUSE
                    STONE BUILDINGS
                    THE GARDENS
                    THE LIBRARY
                    NEW HALL

LINCOLN'S INN FIELDS
GRAY'S INN   INTRODUCTION
                    THE GRIFFIN
                    ENTRANCE
                    SOUTH SQUARE
                    HALL
                    CHAPEL
                    SQUARE
                    FIELD COURT
                    GRAY'S INN WALKS

PROLOGUE

For those who wish to combine information, entertainment and education (the three admitted aims of the B.B.C.), there can be no better guidebook than Tim Daniell's *Inns of Court*. Whether such seekers will emerge with full understanding of the very peculiar and I believe unique English Legal System (or rather lack of system) is anybody's guess. They order matters more logically in Scotland, but presumably members of the American Bar Association know what they are in for. At any rate Tim Daniell keeps them clear of crime because the Central Criminal Court operates in the Old Bailey which is *not* old, built on the site of Newgate which was *not* new, and is outside the quadrilateral of narrow unrestful streets in which the Inns of Court are located. On week days, London traffic roars round Kingsway, Holborn, Gray's Inn Road, Chancery Lane, along the Embankment: Fleet Street roars down its middle. It is comparatively silent on Sunday mornings when the bells of its ancient churches sing through its streets. That is the best time to ramble in company with Tim Daniell.

If a non-legal inexpert, who is nevertheless an experienced London rambler, may give advice to experts, it would be as follows: If you want to savour the atmosphere of our English Legal System, acquire a copy of Anthony Trollope's *Orley Farm* for bedside reading. It was written in 1862 but I do not think the legal profession has changed much since then. Tim Daniell may or may not agree. And if you want to carry away some tangible souvenir of your visit to the Inns of Court, avoid what are described as 'gift shops', look with discriminating eyes on what are offered as 'antiques', and acquire gramophone records of the superb choir which you may hear if your ramble allows you time on a Sunday morning in the Crusaders Church of the Temple. This will enable you to go on hearing it for many a long month, uninterrupted by the roar of London traffic, and the unquiet thought: that time spent in the Temple Church is time filched from something else, that you have come to London to do and probably won't get done.

Mary Stocks

Easter 1971.

THE BARONESS STOCKS, B.SC., LL.D., LITT. D.

LAWYERS

The Law is an exacting mistress. Naturally the world envies the high standard the English lawyer has attained in quest of her demands. In this country there are two strands of lawyer: the advocate proper, the barrister; and the general-practice lawyer, the solicitor. The distinction between the two is that a barrister has the sole right of audience in the High Court.

THE SOLICITOR

By a statute of 1400 lawyers were examined by a judge to verify their competence. In the sixteenth century certain clerks in Chancery acted as advisers to litigants and by the mid-seventeenth century they were admitted to the Roll of Chancery and recognised as being equal to an attorney. And so it developed: the two sides pitched their camps.

Today, a solicitor is a member of a firm through which he is first given his articles. The reputation and practice of the firm is built up by its partners. Whereas a country firm will probably cover the general domestic front ('wives, wills and the rest'), a city firm may specialise on interpretation alone of the Finance Acts. The function of a solicitor is to lend legal advice out of court; if the matter cannot be resolved amicably, it will come before a court of law for impartial adjudication. At this stage the barrister hopes to be briefed.

THE BARRISTER

Veiled in a jealously-guarded yash-mak (Moslem woman's veil), the English Bar retains an anonymity which warrants careful explanation. The English Bar is well proud of its past, but something should here be said of its structure. The Bar comprises a veritable host of advocates whose function is to lend legal expertise in a court of law when called upon to represent a litigant.

Every barrister-aspirant joins one of the four Inns of Court, which has the exclusive privilege of admitting law students to practise advocacy in the Courts of England and Wales. An Inn is akin to a club, the yardstick of which measures the learned in the law. This assembly of advocates eat, sleep (too seldom) and assuredly drink together. The focal point of an Inn is its hall.

To become eligible for Call to the Bar, a law student 'keeps term' in his Inn by 'eating dinner' in hall during the Law Terms. The students arrange themselves down the long wooden benches and share their claret and port with their neighbour. For this purpose the assembly divides itself into messes of four down each table. The 'mess' toasts itself and its neighbours until the evening runs dry. A better custom could never be designed for the mutual acquaintance which a society necessitates. For this reason the Bar, alone among professions, maintains the closest connection between all grades and the young may soon learn the customs, eloquence and friendship of their elders. The Masters of the Bench (Benchers) sit on the High Table, and Barristers on theirs (in seniority). After dinner debates, mock-trials, moots (whence the word 'moot-point' is derived), addresses, and concerts continue. Reading for the Bar also includes examinations, which equip the mind with a training of the memory, much needed in later practice.

These requisites accomplished, the student is then called to the Bar by his Inn: he is published a barrister by the Benchers of his Inn of Court and henceforth authorised to speak from the 'bar' of a court.

Each Inn is governed by the Masters of the Bench (trustees-cum-house committee). From one of their number is chosen a Treasurer, an annual office of 'chairing' the committee. The Benchers are chosen for their eminence, distinguished judges to wit, and men who have otherwise walked successfully upon the platform of public life.

A barrister owes his allegiance to the courts in which he practises. To preserve the interests of justice a barrister must himself remain aloof in professional life. This is achieved by the system of chambers, namely teams of barristers who share their work premises. Business in a set of chambers is conducted through the inconspicuous channel of a clerk, an unqualified person who organises their work. A given set of chambers acquires a reputation: renowned, ignominious or whatever. The better the set, the harder to join.

A fledgling barrister becomes a pupil to a practising member of the Bar for six months after which he may accept a brief in his own right. This is called 'pupillage'. If he impresses the chambers with his aptitude he may be asked to accept a tenancy, i.e. permanently join that set.

QUEEN'S COUNSEL

If a barrister builds up a thriving practice at the Bar, he may decide to 'take silk', that is: to doff his stuff gown and don a silken robe. The Queen confers the status of Queen's Counsel upon the applicant; henceforward he cannot appear in court without a junior. A Junior is a barrister who prepares the case for the silk, just as a surgeon operates only when doctors and anaesthetists have duly prepared the way. The test for employing a silk is: Would a prudent man venture into court with less than two counsel?

It follows that a silk devotes himself to the more serious work. His fees accordingly increase. Taking silk is a precarious step in the career of an advocate and is not recommended to one who walks with an Achilles' heel.

HIGH COURT JUDGES

(Note—Judges of County Courts, Quarter Sessions and lesser courts are not summarised here. To do so would involve an elaboration of the machinery of justice disproportionate to the length of this work.)

If a Queen's Counsel continues to grow in stature, he may be appointed to the Bench. In England, High Court Judges are taken from the nursery of the Bar. In this there is much wisdom: since a Judge's function is to preside over a court of law, who is more suited to fulfil this office than a practitioner who has mastered, over a lifetime, the complexities of court procedure and evidence? Other professions have yet to promise better candidates.

THE ROYAL COURTS OF JUSTICE

Known to Londoners as the Law Courts in the Strand, the High Court was built in 1875 when it moved from Westminster Palace. The project cost £1 million which was paid out of unclaimed funds in Chancery. The architect was G. E. Street, R.A., whose marble statue confronts us within. The High Court covers all the more important civil litigation in England.

'The place of Justice is an hallowed place;
Not only the bench, the precincts ought to be,
Preserved without scandal or corruption;
For grapes will not be gatherd off a thistle tree.'

So wrote Sir Francis Bacon some three hundred years ago. His parchment is faded but not his theme. With 'hallowed sanctity' in mind, inspect now the lofty edifice. The white stonework tolerates the smudges of city fume and lends good contrast to the ornate clock overhanging the Strand. The style is monastic Gothic—well shown by the turrets, which are not used for incarcerating prisoners, as was once assumed by Queen Victoria's subjects.

The interior is now again glorious since its cleaning in 1970 by the Ministry of Works (in league with the Lord Chancellor). The magnificent chamber (238 feet long, 80 feet high) engulfs the spectator as if in some Arthurian legend. The organ-pipe buttresses filter to the sombre ceiling above. Underneath the balcony, far end, is a bust of Queen Victoria who opened the building in 1882; and Lord Russell who displays his stony silence from the hall's perimetre. The statue of Sir William Blackstone was presented by the American Bar Association in 1924.

In the centre is the 'Trial List' which publishes those cases that have reached trial in one of the adjoining court-rooms. The porter at the main entrance will recommend the 'juiciest' of the day. After a pint of beer in the licensed Crypt bar, discover the many passages which afford a worthy inspection of numerous vaulting designs.

Dragon

Wyvern

THE STRAND AND FLEET STREET

At the confluence of these two thoroughfares there once stood an entrance arch to the city of London, known as Temple Bar (see cover). A fearsome dragon menaces this site though as a matter of heraldic fact the supporters of the city's armorial bearings are sometimes wyverns.

Temple Bar was erected in 1672, and was for many years ascribed to Sir Christopher Wren. It is more likely the work of Thomas Knight in conjunction with Joshua Marshall (1629-1678). In 1888, it was bought by Sir Hedworth Meux and removed to his country seat, Theobald's Park, Cheshunt, Herts. Many monarchs have been associated with this grand portal. George III passed through the arch on his return from thanksgiving at St. Paul's for recovering his sanity. It is said that his prayers were premature. Because the city administers its own jurisdiction—it still is, and it is hoped will always remain, a law unto itself—the Lord Mayor in accordance with ancient custom tenders the sword of state, which the Sovereign returns, at one of the city's gates.

The portal was long used for exhibiting to the populace the heads of traitors. This was not to disgrace the dismembered felon still further, but to assure the thirsty mob that the executioner had indeed done a good day's work. The monument straddled the Strand until 1888 when road widening for the new courts sought its despatch to Theobald's Park, where it stands long forgotten to this day. With the abolition of the death penalty the time is ripe for denizens of the Temple to raise the hue and cry for its return.

DOWN THE STRAND

Westwards the 1680 apse of St. Clement Danes, a Wren architectural curtain-raiser leading up to St. Paul's, makes a cleft ear for Dr. Johnson reading from his pedestal, which was erected in 1900 to commemorate the great parishioner. Back and beyond is St. Mary-le-

Dr Johnson & his house

Queen Elizabeth I
(Statue at St. Dunstan's)

Strand, built by James Gibb in 1714, and noted for one of its rectors, Thomas à Becket. Further West, a spiritual appetite is well satisfied by the secular premises of Simpson's Restaurant in the Strand, famed for its traditional English saddle of mutton trolley. The Savoy Hotel adjoins it, built with the profits of the Gilbert & Sullivan operettas, and is situated in the only street of London where you drive on the right. This enabled Mr. D'Oyly Carte's patrons to alight from their carriages at the entrance doors to the Savoy Theatre.

Opposite the Law Courts, note the 'Spy' cartoons in the window of the Wig & Pen Club. Nearby is Messrs. Twining's, the tea merchants who were responsible for the speedy tea-clipper trade to the Far East. At five and twenty past four of an afternoon, a worthy patron, Codrington Edmund Carrington by name, may be encountered (by asking the nice waitress Julia for your introduction to him). His ancestor was the great Chief Justice of Ceylon, the other tea isle, through whom England learnt to drink tea. He welcomes visitors from abroad and readers are recommended to make his acquaintance.

Closeby is to be found the Old Cheshire Cheese, a haven well worth the honour of Dr. Johnson's ghost. The delectable port-wine is most conducive to a full enjoyment of old England.

UP FLEET STREET

Cast your eyes across the roofs that lean over their street facades. This reveals their age more vividly than the shopfronts. The famous 'street of ink' has been associated with printing since 1500 (Caxton's assistant). The Solicitors' Law Stationery Society is where you buy a real writ for five pence. In close view are Coutts Bank (founded in 1692), bankers to Her Majesty the Queen, and Child's (established 1671), bankers to little Nell Gwynne.

The church of St. Dunstan's in the West gave its name to the Home for the Blind, and was mentioned by Dickens in 'The Chimes' of the lantern tower.

Backstage is Dr. Johnson's House (open to the public) at No. 17 Gough Square, where he compiled the great Dictionary. The learned Doctor died in Bolt Court hardby. Marvel at the newspaper superstructures that do so much to belittle the written word; and at the bottom of Fleet Street a stone marks the spot where young Edgar Wallace remained a street newsvendor, till he achieved world renown as a thriller writer.

Down the hill is St. Bride's (alias Bridget, and not of monogamous union), noted for the Roman excavations discovered there after the war. The Church is well associated with the lines of Richard Lovelace: 'Stone walls do not a prison make, nor iron bars a cage . . .'

or the prose: 'I could not love thee dear so much loved I not honour more . . .' Samuel Pepys was baptised here on 3rd March, 1632.

Prince Henry's Room

Beside the Wren church stands a Public House, built by Wren as a dosshouse for his workmen.

The Chanticleer sign that swings over the Cock Tavern replaces the original carved by Grinling Gibbons (and hung inside). Linger awhile at No. 17, Prince Henry's Room, the ancient Council Chamber of the Prince of Wales: it has been well restored by the Greater London Council. The badge of the three feathers finely carved below the upper windows indicates the ancient plaster and panelling within the Chamber, which ceased to keep its secrets when Prince Henry died in 1612. (A report of the Election Case at West Looe, a town in the Royal Duchy of Cornwall, mentions a 'Commission-House in Fleet Street', 25th November, 1635).

CHANCERY LANE

The Lane is named after the ancient writ office (viz. 'Cursitor Street') of the Lord Chancellor, and more especially after the resident Bishop of Chichester, later Chancellor, whose palace was in Lincoln's Inn. This bustling thoroughfare connects Gray's Inn with the other Inns of Court. Until recently, a future occupant of the Woolsack could be espied astride his bicycle en route for luncheon in Lincoln's Inn Hall.

Wending left up the Lane we pass the Law Society to which body all solicitors belong. The building (1832) is protected by iron railings with gilded lions' heads. Opposite, the Public Record Office houses all the historic State Papers, including Domesday (1086) and Magna Carta (1215). On its site stood the Rolls Chapel in which a Bishop once preached the text from Psalm 22 vv. 21: 'Save me from the lion's mouth for thou hast heard me from amongst the horns of the unicorns'. The monarch of the day promptly dismissed the minister of God for levelling against the Royal Arms.

Ede & Ravenscroft, wig and robe makers, have their shop at No. 93, at the back of which Mr. Marsh makes the judges' wigs. Recently a young and impecunious barrister threatened the wig makers with the Monopolies Commission (because wigs are expensive and 'Ede & R' are the only surviving wig-makers in London): 'Delighted', their manager replied, 'let any rival come hither and ease the burden of our orders.' At Star Yard a street lavatory in the Parisian taste often fascinates the passer-by; on the decorative ironwork can be seen the Royal Coat of Arms.

Pass Lincoln's Inn Gate house, and reserve a table with Carlo, the manager of the Forum Restaurant, where the cuisine keeps the gastronomic wolf within its doors. At the top of Chancery Lane are the enormous Silver Vaults which offer a formidable collection of plate and silverware, all for sale.

Knight's Effigy~

THE TEMPLE

Outside the City walls 'in olden days ere witch-craft did begin; before polygamy was made a sin', there grew up a community of warriors. This husbandry distinguished itself from the militia: they dedicated their activities to God's calling, which they interpreted as being their duty to wrest the Holy Land from the Oriental infidel. The avowed aim was to provide Christian pilgrims a free access to Jerusalem.

The site of the Temple was this home of the Crusaders, the Order of the Holy Sepulchre of Knights Templars (whence its name). These strong men chose the close proximity of the city for the obvious protection that an orderly citizenship bestows on its flanks. In medieval times, it must be noted, only the godly or the brave dared live outside a fortification. The Knights' neighbours then included the Whitefriars, the Carmelites, the Blackfriars, the Carthusians at Smithfield, the knights of the Order of St. John at Clerkenwell, and the occasional bishop safely inside his palace. One bishop, His Right Reverence of Exeter, was unhappily beheaded by a cockney mob on his way home to Sunday luncheon in 1326. Times change.

Within the Temple precincts, long before that year, the knights suffered students to read the law. No doubt in so doing they contravened their own ordinance: 'that the Temple Palace be not put to profane uses.' The Temple is situate in the Ward of Farringdon Without, i.e. outside the city wall. Close by Temple Bar, which marked this division, the 'Middle' Temple grew on the verge beside the 'Inner' Temple, inside the city boundary. There was once an Outer Temple westward of the two, since lost to redevelopers.

The scenery of the Temple, in history and beauty, well deserves the label that Ben Jonson gave the Inns of Court: 'the noblest nurseries ... in the Kingdom ?' Before we consider the one time poet laureate's assertion, we must pay just homage to the Temple Church.

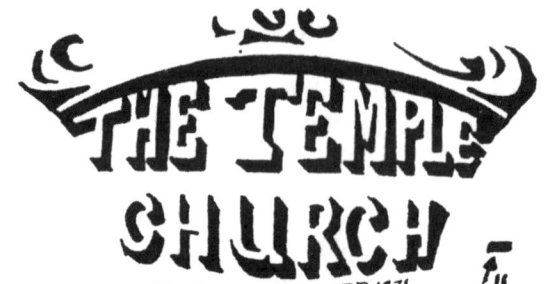

1. PORCH. 2- WEST PORCH & NORMAN DOOR.
3- FONT. 4- KNIGHTS' EFFIGIES 5- ORGAN.
6- STAIR & PENITENTIAL CELL. 7- WREN REREDOS
8- BISHOP'S EFFIGY. 9- SELDEN'S TOMBSTONE
10- PLOWDEN MONUMENT. 11- GOLDSMITH'S TOMB.

THE TEMPLE CHURCH

So far as the scholar concerns himself, he has reached the apex of the Temple: permutation of a millenium. The church is the best surviving example of the Round, the style in which the knights had built wherever their numbers formed a commandery. Commanderies were formed at Little Maplestead in Essex, at Northampton, and at Cambridge—hence the round churches there. A chapel at Rothley Manor near Leicester (now part of an hotel) was also given over to the knights, circa 1140.

When the knights moved to the Temple from the south side of Holborn in 1161, they rightly wished to build a church in the style of St. Sepulchre's, Jerusalem, the apple of their vizered eye. The Temple church was consecrated by the Patriarch Heraclius in 1185. The Patriarch from Jerusalem combined his English mission with a consecration of St. John's church at Clerkenwell. He died that same year— on active service ?

In 1312 the Order was dissolved by the Council of Vienne and its possessions including the church passed to the rival Order of St. John. This Order (of ambulance renown) was founded in 1099 and provided a hospital in Jerusalem for the 'sick and the slain'. Soon its iron hand was turned to the mutual defence of the citadel, its history ending in 1798 when Napoleon captured Malta. (Malta was the last Mediterranean outpost which the knights occupied after their eviction from the Holy Land (1291) and later, from Cyprus and Rhodes.) Since 1800 the Order of St. John has devoted itself to humanitarian needs, a commendable alternative.

In 1540, all these Orders were abolished by King Henry VIII. Only then did the lawyers assume the mantle of Temple ownership.

EXTERIOR

This Normanesque jewel has survived the madness and follies of twentieth-century warfare with miraculous good fortune. The plan comprises the Round, erected in 1185, and the Quire, a subsequent addition of 1240. The fulsome drum of Norman architecture linked to the elegant Early English caverns still resemble its appearance when first erected. The Round illustrates the transitional period of Romanesque (Nave) to the Gothic architecture of the Quire.

The West Porch was copied probably from that at Loges (in France) which the returning Templars had noted on their travels.

The site of the church is thought to have born witness to the Templars' Treasury. This can be well imagined by observing the West Porch, with its chunky mouldings and peering down the maze of steps below the railings.

Goldsmith ~ R·I·P~

On the north side of the church, Oliver Goldsmith's simple tomb (1774) contrasts with the monument to one Johannes Hiccocks alongside. The black stanchion rising from the paving defines the boundary of the two Inns: MT, Middle to the North; IT, Inner to the South.

INTERIOR

The cylindrical Round is embroidered by six thin clerestory windows. Six Purbeck marble pillars hang like iron drapery. They disguise their true purpose: to bolster the weight of the dome. On closer inspection, the columns are seen to lean four inches outwards from the centre—akin to the umbrella frame principle. Consider the builders' achievement in transporting the marble from the Dorset quarries all those years ago.

The slumbering crusaders snore in full armour of whom the cross-legged William Marshall, 4th Earl of Pembroke, looks the most comfortable for this backbreaking feat. Eastwards the Quire is seen to advantage. It comprises three equal aisles once set on tiled pavement 'oft repeated with emblems of the Temple'. The eye is drawn to the reredos screen, designed by Sir Christopher in 1682. The screen was removed to the Bowes Museum (co. Durham), by

Victorian 'restorers' in the last century, but it returned home unscathed after the war.

Inspect the sanctuary chairs which guard the Altar; they illuminate the banners of the two societies handsomely—the paschal lamb bears its cross to the northside, the tail of the pegasus to the south. The chairs are so placed to denote the division of the church since the Deed of Partition in 1732. The organ is a technical 'tour de force'; George Thalben-Ball praises the three 32 foot stops—praise indeed!—; whereas Westminster Abbey has but two. The original organ was chosen by the musical ear of Judge Jeffreys, after a year of intense feud between the rival organ-makers: Smith and Harris. Throughout that year Purcell fugued for Father Smith (who caught the judicial ear) and Queen Caroline's organist harassed for Harris.

In the South aisle are situate:

A grand effigy of a bishop, in mint condition and identified as the Patriarch Heraclius (a theory since discounted by modern historians);

The unusual plaque of Witham, Baronetti—this did not denote Italian blood in an English Baronet necessarily, for it was the custom of the age to write in Latin.

Ye Lady Morton, a person 'orthodox and exemplary for . . . chastity, constancy, and patient suffering with her husband';

Ann Littleton's tombstone: 'For while this jewel here is set, this grave is but a cabinet;'

And Selden's tomb (1654) stirs beneath the glass slab in the floor.

Seek out the stair leading to the penitential cell (in the triforium). A disobedient Templar was confined to this dress circle seat, only to hear his virtuous brothers incantate beneath him till he passed away. Among the pinioned arches and the freestone effigies contemplate the setting: 'And on his bust a bloudie cross he bore;
           the dear remembrance of his dying Lord' (Spencer). After a short prayer it behoves us to become acquainted with the Middle Temple.

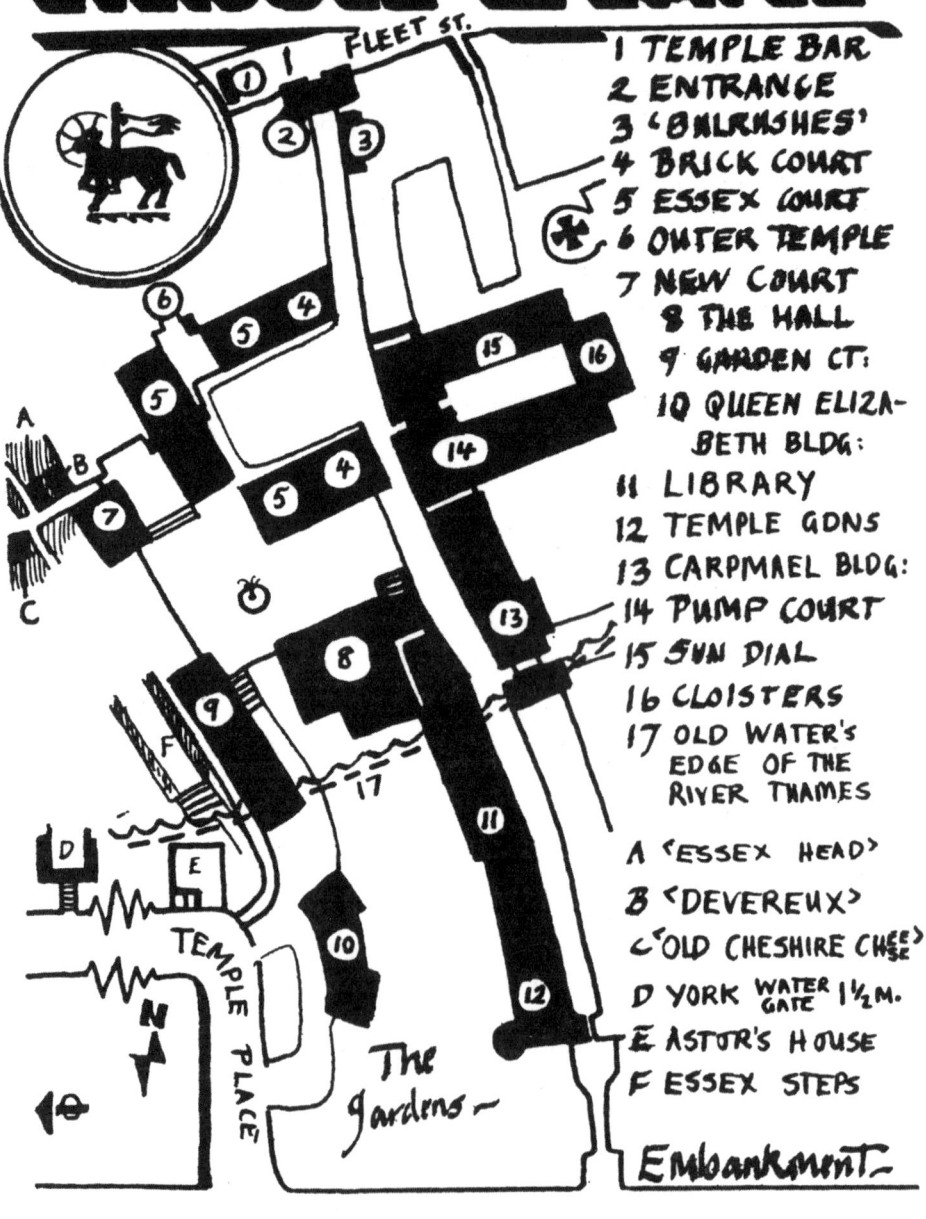

THE MIDDLE TEMPLE

HISTORY

The oldest records that exist of the Honourable Society of the Middle Temple stem from 1501. These records were called 'Domus' and confirm that the four Inns of Court had then become well established as 'secular monasteries'. The lawyers (later, 'barristers-at-law') are thought to have first settled in the Temple in the fourteenth century.

The Middle Temple commands an important place in the hall of fame, as a cursory list of its distinguished members will show:

Of Lawyers; Lord Chancellors: Clarendon, Somers, Hardwicke, Eldon, Sankey and Jowitt. Lord Chief Justices: Cockburn, Coleridge, and Reading. Also Sir William Blackstone, Lords Stowell, Brampton (Alias Sir Henry Hawkins who inspired the music hall song 'I'm 'Enery 'Awkins'), Lords Lindley, Phillimore, Carson, du Parcq, and Scrutton.

Of literature; John Evelyn, Henry Fielding, William Cowper, Richard Sheridan, Thomas de Quincey, William Makepeace Thackeray, Charles Dickens, and John Buchan (later Lord Tweedsmuir).

Of patriots; Sir Francis Drake, Sir Walter Raleigh, Sir Martin Frobisher, Sir John Hawkins, Edmund Burke, and one John Dickinson who drafted the Declaration of Independence (of the signatories who adopted it, five were Middle Templars).

THE PASCHAL LAMB

When the Order of the Knights Templars was founded, heraldry was in its infancy. The Society of the Middle Temple adopted or continued to bear the badge that had been assigned to the Templars: namely, Agnus Dei, a paschal lamb holding the banner of innocence, set in a red cross on a white nimbus ground. This design is a favourite Christian symbol to be seen on many Near East monuments.

The reader is recommended to inspect each building in the Temple and identify it, by the lamb, as belonging to the Middle Temple, or the pegasus of the Inner. The more usual place to find the badge is over a doorway, or on a rain-water head. The Author has discovered the lamb even in a water closet, one example of Victorian embellishment or Judicial fatigue.

Middle Temple: Wren Entrance~

MIDDLE TEMPLE LANE

The imposing gatehouse to the Middle Temple can be seen to advantage from the far side of Fleet Street. The facade was designed by Wren in 1684 and replaced an earlier archway built and paid for by Sir Amias Pawlet. The diaryist John Aubrey adds: Pawlet's gesture was less than generous: he paid in settlement of a fine levied by Cardinal Wolsey! Inside those old gates there used to be seen the scars made by an old iron bar, placed when Wat Tyler threatened the Temple with his presence in 1381.

> 'As by the Templars' holds you go
>   the Horse and Lamb displayed,
> In emblematic figures show
>   the merits of their trade.
> That clients may infer from thence,
>   how just is their profession,
> The Lamb sets forth their innocence,
>   the Horse their expedition.
> Oh Happy Britons! Happy Isle!
>   Let foreign nations say—
>   Where you get justice without guile, and Law without delay.'

This rhyme was pinned on the gates in 1774.

Passing through the centre arch, the closeby cloister diverts the traveller: it is said that Dr. Johnson on his way to chambers would kiss the black supports that resemble iron bulrushes. No more do we hear the muffin man (so liked by Dickens) nor the porter winding (blowing) his horn, but for a quiet moment we can embrace this atmosphere and think with Charles Lamb: 'a man would give something to be born in such places . . .'

BRICK AND ESSEX COURT

This court opens to the west and is a uniform example of barristers' sets of chambers. Spenser alluded to Brick Court as 'those bricky towers' although the present buildings date from 1882. At No. 2 resided Oliver Goldsmith who died there in 1774 (see tomb, Temple Church). Thackeray writes of weeping women filling the stair within the black oak door when the 'greatest and most generous of all men' passed away. Another denizen, Edmund Burke, followed the women's example by bursting into tears; Sir Joshua Reynolds laid aside his brushes for the day. The only person that showed less emotion was Sir William Blackstone who, living beneath, had complained 'of the constant racket above'. Perhaps 'the racket' which interrupted the Commentaries was caused by Goldsmith's

landlady, as Dr. Johnson explains: 'I received one morning an urgent message from poor G. (Goldsmith) and went accordingly as soon as I was dressed. His landlady had arrested him for his rent at which he was in a violent passion. I put the cork into the madeira bottle, desired he would be calm, and seeing he had a book ready for the publisher, looked into it and saw its merits. Telling the lady I should soon return I sold it to the bookseller for sixty pounds. G. duly discharged his rent but not without rating his landlady in a high voice for having used him so ill . . .'

NEW COURT

The reader arrives at New Court by walking through the passage in Essex Court building (west). Notice the forty-five-rung ladder which is chained to the wall of the passage: does the law protect buildings from fire or chattels from thieves?

New Court was designed by Wren after the Middle Temple acquired part of the garden belonging to the Devereux family. (The public house 'Devereux' recalls the surname of the Earls of Essex.)

The metal emblems on the white stucco walls were displayed by the Georgian house-owner so that the insurance company in question could easily identify his burning building. Amongst others, '51906' is a policy number, and the 'portcullis' or 'three feathers' the badge of a company. The earliest Fire Marks were of lead and date from 1667, supplanted in the nineteenth century by tin or copper Fire Plates—brightly painted and used solely for advertisement. This prompted an Hanoverian rhyme:

'For not even the Regent himself has endured,
—though I've seen him with badges and orders all shine—
Till he looked like a house that was over-insured.' (1816.)

Down the steps and we enter Garden Court which faces the Middle Temple Gardens.

MIDDLE TEMPLE GARDENS

Rendered immortal by Shakespeare in Henry VI, part I, the reader will also remember that the Wars of the Roses began with Lord Suffolk suggesting:

'Within the Temple Hall we were too loud,
The garden here is more convenient . . .'

Quick to the cause Warwick rejoins:

'I love no colours—and without all colour
Of base insinuating flattery,
I pluck this white rose with Plantagenet . . .' and he now

becomes sparring partner to the Duke of York. To make up a foursome, the quorum for all good games, Suffolk intervenes: 'I pluck this red rose with young Somerset'. The Shakespearean word 'colour' was taken to mean deceit, rather as modern English uses the phrase 'colourable' pretext. Thus the fatal civil war was conceived upon the casual choice of two Temple roses.

Before the Victorian Embankment was built (1865), the gardens of the two societies merged with one another and the Temple Pier gave busy countenance to the River Thames which, thanks to the motorcar, it has now lost.

Time permitting, a stroll to Essex Steps is rewarding. The superb Water-Gate built in the garden of Essex House (demolished) was designed by Wren. Across the river, half London is in your pocket; up the street the Strand disects the shadows of the High Court.

No. 2 Temple Place was the toy of the 1st Viscount Astor, well restored after the war. Built in 1895 by Pearson (of Truro Cathedral), the date was an indication that m'lord had inherited enough Canadian beavers to consider the luxuries of life in London. The Portland stone handiwork is pleasing as is the weather-vane: a caravel, the ship that took Christopher Columbus to the Americas.

QUEEN ELIZABETH BUILDING

This block of chambers, named after Queen Elizabeth the Queen Mother, is a recent addition to the Middle Temple brotherhood. It stands adjacent to the site of the old Middle Temple Library, the wall of which now supports some garages. By withtracing your steps, Fountain Court emerges in the sun.

FOUNTAIN COURT

Under the shade of the very old mulberry tree, inspect the idle carp basking in the pool. There were nineteen incumbents when last counted, albeit in 1896. This is the perimeter of essayist pleasure as Dickens discovered:

'Brilliantly the Temple fountain sparkled in the sun, as little Ruth and her companion came towards it. There Tom would see her, not sauntering you understand, but coming briskly up, with the best little laugh upon her face that ever played in opposition to the fountain. The fountain might have leaped up twenty feet to greet this spring of hopeful maidenhood that in her person stole through the dry and dusty channels of the law . . .'

Having counted the goldfish, gaze across the hazy Thames, with pulp barges at rest on the south bank mud like slumbering hippopotami. This promontory leads to:

Ruth & Tom's Winter in Fountain Court.

THE MIDDLE TEMPLE HALL

In 1562 the lawyers of the long evenings decided to build themselves a gorgeous hall which Queen Elizabeth I opened in 1576. The design resembles that of Trinity, Cambridge, (of contemporary construction). The roof distinguishes itself amongst the finest in the world. It is spanned by Elizabethan double hammerbeams now 400 years old.

The gothic windows lend a masterful if incongruous touch to the superb structure. . In 1572 glass was still as expensive as salt, a commodity zealously guarded by the glaziers, reliant wholly on the monopoly of the glass-blower. For this reason alone, among structural others, a window was a means of showing off precious coloured mineral, and not an aperture which it is today because the old problem of heating has been solved.

The Interior shows a worthy elegance: the end by which you enter is highlighted by a richly carved screen (1574). Its origin was wrongly attributed to a Spanish galleon that foundered on our shores in 1588 along with the Papist Armada. Allow the eye to roam round the tuscan columns and note the anticipation of the Palladian style, so early, so handsome, so good.

The screen vies with an elephant for sheer memory: In 1601 it is commonly spoken that Shakespeare, at Candlemas, acted here in 'Twelfth Night'. The performance would have been conducted from the dais at the far end of the hall on which there rests the High Table, a gift from the one and only Virgin Queen Elizabeth I. Of oak from Windsor Park, it was floated down the Thames to Temple Pier. History alleges that the death warrant for Mary Queen of Scots was signed on its mellow surface.

Below the dais stands a smaller but no less distinguished table. The members call it the cup-board and it was made from the timbers of the Golden Hind (the ship of Sir Francis Drake, a Middle Templar, lest we forget). The armour that always embroidered the hall was a worthy vestige of the knights, a token of history as authentic as the panels that bear the Arms of the Readers. The portraits from left to right are of:

> Queen Elizabeth I (alcove)
> Queen Anne
> King Charles II
> King Charles I (school of Van Dyke)
> King James II
> King William III.

THE MIDDLE TEMPLE SILVER

The vaults of the Middle Temple house a rare and beautiful collection of silver to be enjoyed only under the ever-watchful eye of Master Stranger Jones. The chief benefactor was the first Viscount Rothermere (whose brother Viscount Northcliffe master-minded the revolution of the Popular Press). Octogenarian Benchers recall that Rothermere—an honorary Bencher himself—would arrive for luncheon with parcels discreetly wrapped in brown paper (and not, as some fondly recount, in the latest edition of the 'Daily Mail'). Even austere lawyers lost their decorum when the contents were revealed—in all some twenty-five choice items of Tudor, Jacobean and Commonwealth Silver, all dated within the years 1558-1658. These and the Harmsworth law scholarships were given by Rothermere in memory of his father, Alfred Harmsworth, a barrister of the Society.

an item of Middle Temple Silver:
silver gilt standing salt, of 1565.

PUMP COURT

A quick reference to the map will show the strategic position of this courtyard in times of emergency. Fire pumps were stationed around this yard, hence its name. (There is a disused well on the site.) A fire broke out in 1678 which devoured more of the Temple buildings than the Great Fire itself, twelve years earlier. Not even the butteries of the nearby hall that spurted barrels of quenching beer into the pumping engines could avert the havoc: the night was freezing; the water supply frozen.

Do not miss the sun-dial with the caption: 'Shadows we are and like shadows we depart'—an untimely reminder to us all. It is told that Judge Jeffreys resided here. The message on the sun-dial did not presume to be an oracle, even to the 'bloody' judge.

THE CLOISTERS

The Wren Cloister showing the false columns.

The cloisters are uninteresting. They reconstruct with cold gaiety those from Wren's pencil, destroyed in May, 1941. When the Benchers approved the great architect's work in 1681 they marvelled that a few elegant columns could support the full weight of the rooms above. (Perhaps it was their collective weight, since they frequented the rooms.) To appease their discomfort, Wren inserted into his plan a second row of centre columns. The happy Benchers concurred. They never knew the truth! The extra columns stopped short of the ceiling by one inch; indiscernible to the eye at ground level.

Sir Edward Maufe was chosen to be the Middle Temple's post-war architect. His drawings for the Middle Temple, we learn, were inadvertently lost to the University of Pennsylvania last year (for a 'four figure sum'). It occurred when the distinguished architect was moving house; dustmen were paid to remove a stack of papers. Included in these were the Temple drawings. Delight that these historical manuscripts were saved depends upon which side of the Atlantic you were born.

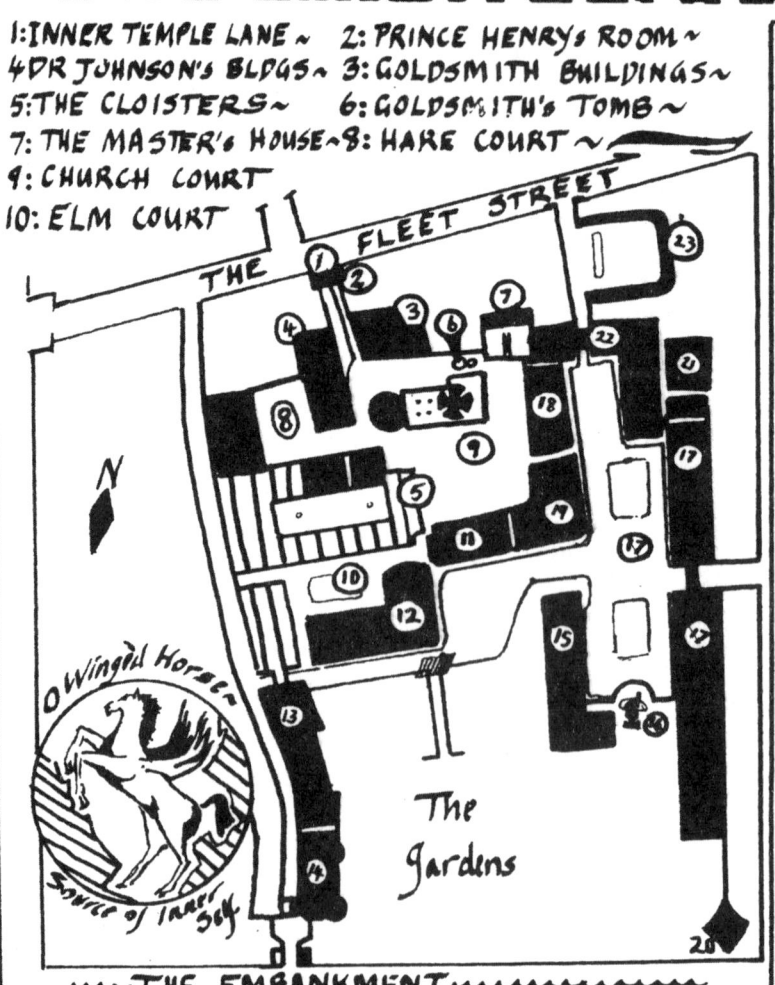

THE INNER TEMPLE

The reader will recall why the Inner Temple assumed its name, but not the reason for a second society. The community grew and grew, larger and larger, until it overflowed into its own back-garden, behind the Templars' original house. The Inner represents the colony of 'students of the law' who first settled themselves in the premises of the old Orders of Chivalry.

One wag has compared the Middle Temple to a beautiful bride and the Inner to her dull husband. It is a trite comparison. It is more likely that the 700-year-old couple have imbued each other with more grace than the misogamist wag.

The Paston Papers refer to the Inner Temple as a separate society in 1440 (1st October). In Canterbury Tales, Chaucer alludes to a
'gentil manciple was there of Temple,
Of whom achatours mighten take ensample'
The manciple bought 'vitaille' for a godly number of 'maisters' (more than thrice ten) 'that were in law expert and curious'.

In 1340 King Edward III gave the property to the Prior of St. John. The Lord Prior was allowed to collect faggots, 1000 p.a., from Lilleston Woods, which sinecure brought forth no doubt the Prior's prayers in the Royal adventures abroad. (Lilleston Woods or 'Lisson' Grove is known to Londoners as St. John's Wood.)

In 1505 the archives of the society began their good work which continues to the present day. In 1608 King James I granted the society the limited ownership of the site. In gratitude, a delegation of benchers hustled down the Strand to Whitehall and presented the sovereign with a 'stately cup' of pure gold. They would have done better to refrain from such flattery, for the King's son pawned it on the last of his European holidays.

In 1675 the Society purchased full title for £78. By a quirk in land law the property became vested in the benchers of the Middle Temple. The tiff was resolved by the deed of Partition, drawn up in 1732, since which time the respective parties have lived together as gentlemen, sometimes, do.

The Inner Temple has bred an illustrious army of men:
Sir Thomas Littleton (author of the treatise on Tenure); Sir John Pakington, another Worcestershire Templar known to history as the old man who was allowed to wear his hat, because of 'age and

infirmity' in the substantial presence of King Henry VIII; Sir Edward Coke, Chief Justice of the King's Bench, 'father' of the Common Law; Sir Julius Caesar, Master of the Rolls (1614); Sir Heneage Finch, later Lord Nottingham—one of the 'black finches' of Kensington, because of their dark countenance; John Selden, antiquarian; Thurlow, Lord Chancellor; George Grenville, Prime Minister 1763; Lord Ellenborough; Lord Erskine; Goddard, Lord Chief Justice; Charles Lamb—'Bring your glass and I will show you the Surrey hills from my bed'; Baron Maseres; William Cowper who lived here until he was removed to an asylum at St. Albans in 1600; and Boswell who entered as a student in 1765.

THE PEGASUS

It will be recalled that the knights took their vows of poverty, chastity, and obedience very seriously—that is, before the spoils of victory taught them safer principles. The 'Beausant' banner they chose embodied these virtues three in one: the vow of poverty was explained by two knights riding one horse; the vow of chastity was met by the filly taking flight if compromised; the vow of obedience was dutifully observed by one knight on horseback rescuing another from the field of battle.

Thus the Inner Temple developed its emblem in heraldry: 'azure, a horse bearing two men, argent'. By and by the 'hoss' took flight and ditched the two worthy knights.

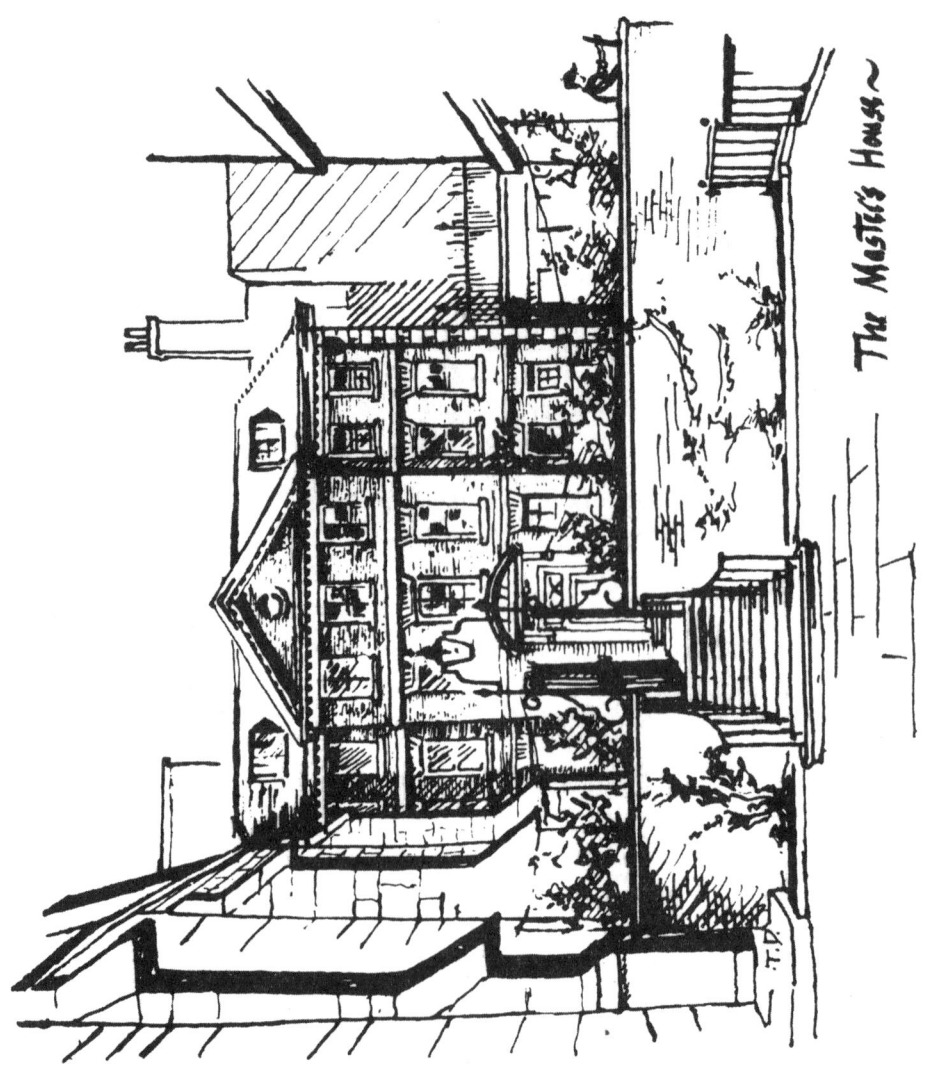

The Masters House

INNER TEMPLE LANE

This modest aperture to Fleet Street wanders to the courtyard of the Temple Church. Here William Blackstone stepped on his way to the gardens, there to read poetry (or, as he tells us): 'to be sacrificed to the muses'. Dr. Johnson resided in the building on the right, 1760-65, and it is off this lane where Boswell first met him. A week later his literary accomplice records, in vivid broadside, one of Johnson's recurring dilemmas:

'On Madame de Boufflers leaving, a sound like thunder descended and J. overtook her. On a little recollection he had taken it into his head to do her the honour of his literary residence.'

We may wonder at the lady's departure for Murphy described Dr. J. as living 'mostly in poverty, total idleness and the pride of literature'. Or we may read of Ozia Humphrey's account:

'As J. sat raving over his breakfast like a lunatic, I could hardly help thinking him a madman. Dress'd in w'stco't, breeches also brown, although they had been crimson, and an old black wig; everything he says is as correct as a second edition; 'tis almost impossible to argue with him as he is so sententious and knowing.'

Glance back up the lane to the newsvendor Mr. Cole, who makes a colourful pose as the author's good friend; he sells the guide.

In the derelict Hare Court, Judge Jeffreys had his chambers.

THE MASTER'S HOUSE

Built by Wren after the Great Fire, the original house was destroyed by incendiaries in 1941. The Master resides herein by authority of Letters Patent under the Great Seal. It is in the gift of the Crown, a vestige from the time when the Crown owned the Temple. The present replica is a conscientious rebuilding much enhanced by the embracing foliage of wistaria, magnolia and passion flower. The iron railings in the foreground are kissed by the hedge of roses and the Master, Canon Milburn, reveals to the horticultural reader that albertine is an easy grower.

'Looking with pleasure on the monuments and epitaphs', as Pepys was doing in 1666, we leave the Master's House for the Inner Temple Hall, opposite.

THE INNER TEMPLE HALL

This, the third of the halls to stand on this site, replaced that of Sydney Smirke in 1952, and was designed by Sir Hubert Worthington. Its run of the mill exterior deceives the eye: there are many treasures within. The windows are graceful reconstructions of the Restoration period but only a modern architect would design them not to open!

Seven centuries' pageantry of Readers' armorial bearings line the panelling inside the hall. Each Treasurer in his year of office leaves his family identity to the notice of less distinguished brethren who dine there in the law terms. A painting by Romney is well worth the minutes spent finding it, which is more than can be said for a cardboard portrait of Prince Philip, a Patron of the society.

At the far end of the hall is the Benchers' Table where the late Geoffrey Tyndale Q.C. was known for his healthy appetite, though he rarely partook of the main course. A Bencher is entitled to the 'common fares' which means he can eat freely all, except the main dish (which Benchers must pay for). Mr. Tyndale—thank you very much—never had room for the main; and Mr. Tyndale was respected at the Bar.

Continuing along this line of buildings we pass the Inner Temple Treasury, the administrative centre of the Inn. The Sub-Treasurer delights to show the privileged visitor the Pegasus carved by Grinling Gibbons rescued from the burning hall in 1941. The library dwells on the corner and is clothed with 90,000 volumes including some of Coke C. J.'s manuscripts and the Petyt collection (formed by the Keeper of the Tower of London).

The better-known collection of Selden was foolishly lost to the Bodleian at Oxford. On the site of the Library stood the Templar's Strong Room, a sort of Plantagenet Bank of England. Indeed Edward I stole some of its holy treasure because he felt like 'seeing to his mother's jewellery!' Some mothers have them—sons and jewellery.

CROWN OFFICE ROW

By the arch, metal rings used to be visible, a legacy predating the Thames embankment when barges tethered here.

Charles Lamb was born in this 'place of my kindly engender' in 1775, as the plaque records. Sir Charles Wheeler designed the Pegasus over the doorway to No. 2 which should be compared to the weather vane on the tiles. Its aged twin spanned the Hall's roof until in the bombing raids of 1941 it took flight (but was recaptured later).

The Society has a photograph recording this unusual manoeuvre which the Sub-Treasurer is obliged to treasure. Do not miss the medieval butteries which are buried in the foundations of the hall (west and overlooking Elm Court). A fifteenth-century fireplace of the original hall is accessible to the enterprising. The lead guttering in Elm Court shows off the Temple's crests handsomely, though the distasteful net curtains in the third storey window do not befit a Temple resident.

INNER TEMPLE GARDENS

The proud wrought-iron gates invite the eye's inspection of the motifs: the pegasus accompanied by the Gray's Inn griffin, which betokens the accord between the two Inns. Gray's Inn presented the gates to the Honourable Society in 1730. This silhouette honours the meandering outline of the Temple architecture, clean and clear, against the King's Reach of the Thames beyond the treeline. The pond dilutes the contours of the moist lawn and the plinth boasts the unbelievable words: 'Lawyers were children once'—some still are.

A much more tempting sun-dial than the little one on the near terrace is found within the shadows of Paper Buildings. The blackamoor balances his platter thus:

'In vain poor sable son of woe,
   Thou see'st the tender tear;
From cannibals thou fledst in vain,
   Lawyers less quarter give;
The first won't eat you till you're slain,
   The last will do it alive'.

The statue was probably cast at one of the Piccadilly statuaries, circa 1700; its birth in Italy is attractive conjecture.

It was here that Bencher Barrington, in the annals of Charles Lamb, was reputed to practise his pretensions as a naturalist, until the following episode finished him: 'Having disbursed 20/- for stuff to poison the sparrow with', the society refused to refund him.

Carrington recounts the story of another bencher, Judge Jeffreys, who 'oft walked the gardens before breaking fast'. On one such morn m'lud encountered the head gardener and by way of conversation remarked: 'With one stroke of my cane, his head will roll'. The Judge was referring to a daisy on the lawn. 'Agh y' onor. it beed a wrong sod to lay low' said the gardener wisely; after all, his own head was far too close for a grammatical error of providence.

PAPER BUILDINGS

'Of building strong albeit of paperweight' (Spencer) it is academic to choose (because it burnt down in 1838) between the two theories of its derivation: whether being of the early timber-plaster construction; or whether it owed its name to the paperwork consumed therein (in which event it is not surprising that it burnt so quickly). Its cold attire is the mark of its architect, Smirke... When the site was being rebuilt a mason asked the Treasurer for any apt couplet on the consecration stone. Dismissing the umpteenth question as a daily technicality the hon. gentleman snapped 'Be gone about your business'—his comment adorns the plaster evermore (can you find it ?).

HARCOURT BUILDINGS AND TEMPLE GARDENS BUILDINGS

The symmetrical chunk that punctuates the west verge of the gardens is named after Lord Chancellor Harcourt; the canopied white stone of Temple Gardens Buildings treads near the water of the Thames and was designed by Sir Charles Barry, architect of the Houses of Parliament, that may be seen in the distance.

KING'S BENCH WALK

Imposing chambers fumble past the cobbled square to the eastern perimeter of the Temple. The doorways reflect the detail of a more gracious age when the purpose of architecture was to improve the landscape of which it deprived nature. In this instance Wren weighs elegant improvisation on 'the doorway' theme. At No. 3 was the Alienation Office which collected the fines levied on land held of the Crown ('alienated'). Hidden nearby is Niblett Hall now used for examinations from which our age shows its uncertainty in judging fellow men.

At No. 5 resided Lord Mansfield, Chief Justice, in his ermine robes as mentioned by Pope:

> 'Graced as thou art with all the power of words,
> So known, so honoured in the House of Lords'

and parodied by Colley Cibber:

> 'Persuasion tips his tongue whene'er he talks:
> And has his chambers in the King's Bench Walks' (1720).

MITRE COURT BUILDINGS

The view bestows the loveliest vista in the Inn, as Lamb beseeches ! 'Tis the most elegant spot in the metropolis.' The terse 1830 facade does not waste brick beyond its strict necessity, a feature of Neo-Classicism. The archway opens to Sergeant's Inn, flamboyant in its caged courtyard which is renowned for Elvino's Wine Bar, a refuge to the knowing lawyer (who refers to it as the 'library'), but bookworms will know better.

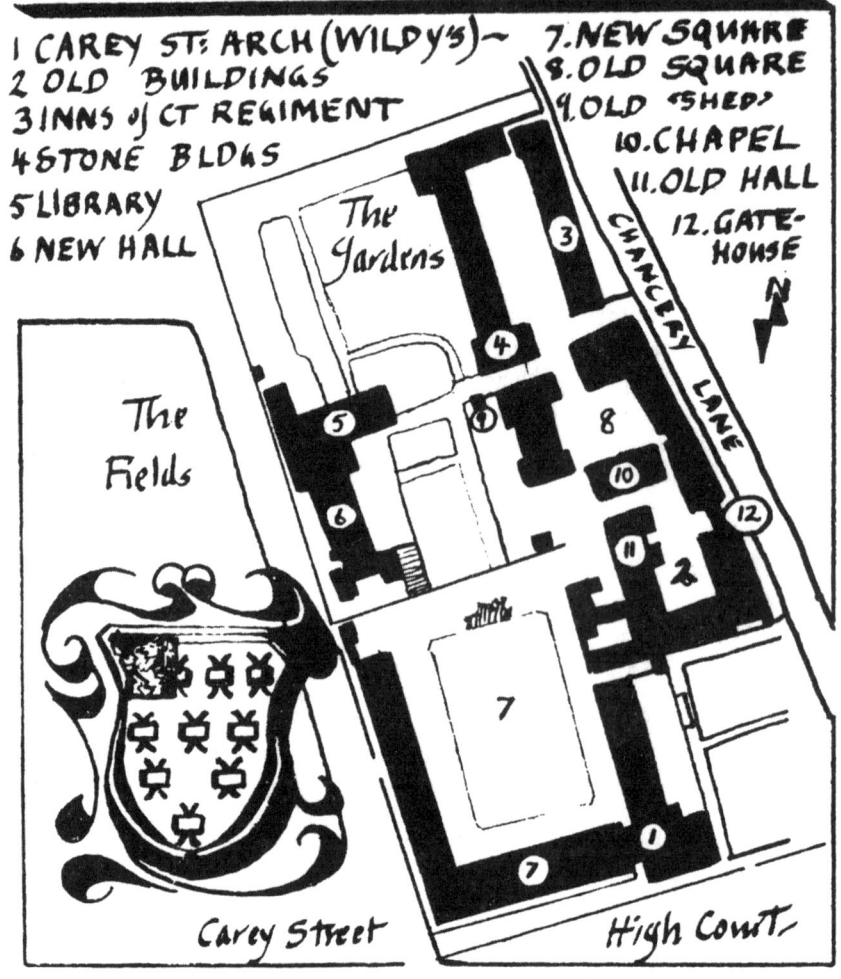

LINCOLN'S INN

INTRODUCTION

It will be recalled that the Templars began their association with the Temple when they removed from Holborn, which premises they had outgrown. They also obtained a meadow on the other side of the Strand, called Fickett's Field. This open space was doubtless used for sharpening their wits on horseback. By and by the 'Friars Preachers' who had settled in this vicinity left for Blackfriars, and sold the site to the Earl of Lincoln, in 1286. It appears that these acres were rich in herb gardens—a fact we may believe if we note that the great liqueurs now popularly drunk originated from the orchards of monastic communities, e.g. Commanderia, Chartreuse, Benedictine, etc.

It is probable that the Earl found the company of lawyers a convenient 'block-booking' for his extensive premises for upon his death in 1311 they began their permanent tenure. In 1536 the Bishop of Chichester ceased to reside in his palace off Chancery Lane, named as was noted earlier in our excursion, after the last resident Bishop who was Chancellor of England in 1292 and 1307. Only in 1580 did the Benchers of the Honourable Society of Lincoln's Inn obtain the freehold title.

The Black Books of the society refer to the Inn's existance in 1422 and are a unique record of history to the present day. They may be inspected by arrangement with the Librarian and other powers that be.

MEMBERS OF THE SOCIETY

The list of great lawyers cuts through history, with names such as: Sir Thomas More; Lord Keeper Egerton (later Lord Ellesmere); Richard Cromwell; Sir Matthew Hale, who entered as a student in 1626; Earl of Mansfield, called to the Bar in 1730; Lord Chancellor Bathurst; Lords Campbell, St. Leonards, Brougham, Eldon, Erskine, Lyndhurst, and Fortescue: and to date, Denning, M. R.; Parker, L. C. J.; and Hailsham, L. C.

Of famous men: John Donne; Tillotson; Warburton; Hurd; Heber; Horace Walpole who entered as a student in 1731; William Penn; William Pitt; Macaulay; Rider Haggard; President Eisenhower and Dean Acheson of the U.S.A.

THE ARMS OF THE SOCIETY

The coat of arms of the society was certified in 1701 by the Herald's

Office, and still are, 'azure seme de fers de miline or on a dexter canton' 'or a lion rampant purpurs'; the lion springs from the de Lacy family.

ENTRANCE CAREY STREET ARCH

Looking at the Inn through the well-protected arch, tempts the visitor to remain in Carey Street. This is inadvisable for its name is still synonymous with the Bankruptcy Court. The arch was once a carriageway flanked by two covered footpaths—the Duke of Wellington found the entrance handy when in 1830 he outwitted a London mob who had chased him and his right wing opinions from the city. In 1832 Wildy's, law booksellers, took a tenancy and it makes a delightful warehouse for the legal bookworm. Ornate coats of arms with the treasurer's initials may be seen above the arch.

NEW SQUARE

The centre of the Square was long the witness of the Execution block; but this ceased in 1620. By 1693 in opposition to Dr. Barbon (the son of 'Praise God Barebones'), Henry Serle built Serle's Court. In 1830

the garden replaced a Corinthian column centre-piece and the square assumed its present character. Overlooking the square, a statue of Queen Victoria cast by J. E. Thomas (and thought to be

the first in her reign) used to peer from the south gable but has since been removed (R.I.P.). The fine gates that lock up the garden were saved from being melted into ammunition in 1940, unlike the railings that once surrounded the square.

OLD HALL

The oldest building of Lincoln's Inn is the Old Hall, which replaced the Bishop's hall in 1489. Though discarded by the society when the New Hall project was launched in 1845, this structure offers the traveller the kindest response to his visit. It has since served as a

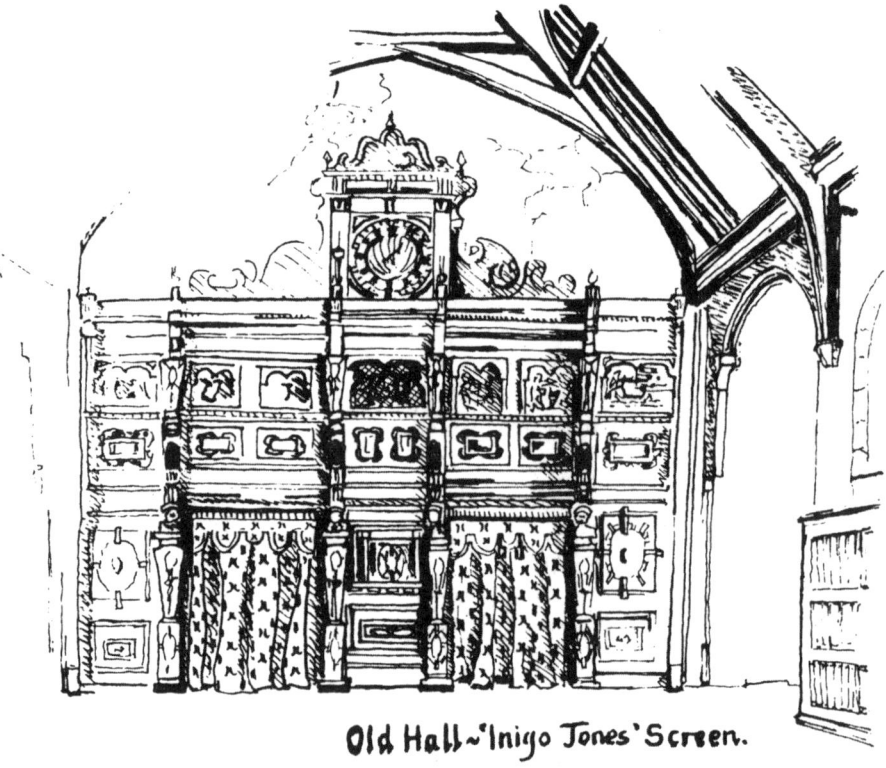

Old Hall – 'Inigo Jones' Screen.

chapel, a lecture hall, and before the Law Courts had been built in the Strand, the Chancellor held his court within. Many a litigant (viz. Jarndyce v. J: Bleak House) must have glazed gloomily at the Hogarth painting: 'St. Paul Before Felix', above the ashern judges' wigs. The picture was commissioned in 1748, was restored in 1970, Felix was the Roman Governor of Caesarea (The Acts, ch. 24, vv. 24/5). The captions that appeared with a contemporary print are curious: 'design'd and scratch'd in the true Dutch taste, in the rediculous manner of Rembrandt'.

The saga of the scroll (in Felix's right hand) is of interest: Hogarth first painted the scroll actually dropping from the Roman's grip. Receiving an anonymous letter—'so offended at the scroll in mid-air' the artist altered its locus to the present and more comfortable position. The rich brushwork exemplifies the gift of this great English artist; namely, the elusive skill of injecting onto canvas the full emotion that swells from man's face in anguish.

Notice before you leave for the Chapel how decorative is the uncommon screen awash with drapery, once attributed to Inigo Jones.

THE CHAPEL

Ordered in the year 1609 and built in 1623 it replaced an earlier 'insufficient and ruinous' place of worship. The Dean of St. Paul's preached the first sermon there on Ascension Day. Such was the crowd that many were taken up for dead (of whom it is hoped that their departing choice of Calendar Day was auspicious). The exterior Gothic is improvised in Inigo Jones and was much altered by Wyatt in 1797 and by Salter in 1882. The open-plan crypt affords a daylight inspection of worn burial tombs. Stow in his survey recounts: 'A pleasing melancholy by night that may be felt but not described' (1755), which leaves little more to be said. The rare stained glass windows in the body of the Chapel are the work of Bernard Van Linge, who was commissioned by friends of Shakespeare no less.

OLD BUILDINGS

This courtway frames the reconstructed Gate-house opening on to Chancery Lane. It was built to extend the forecourt of the Gatehouse 1534-1613, by the making of 'a bevy of new chambers at the back side' of the hall. The pleasing fragments of Tudor brick denote by their age the many distinguished residents among whom was Cromwell's Secretary of State, Thurloe, who lived at No. 24 and later at No. 13. His State Papers were discovered in a false ceiling in the reign of William III. The ubiquitous 'Dizzy' (Benjamin Disraeli) also found time to live in this square before he aspired to Downing Street. Another resident was John Donne, the Christian who aspired to a sound eminence of straightforward Christian teaching.

His inspiration was his 'cherry-love' Anne, with whom he eloped. She was the niece of the Chancellor to whom he was secretary. No sooner did 'uncle' (later Lord Ellesmere) discover his young secretary's commitment than nephew-in-law was dismissed. This resulted in the famous line: 'John Donne, Anne Donne, Un-done ;'

THE GATE HOUSE

Built in 1517 of bricks baked in the Inn's coneygarth (brick-kiln), its completion was entrusted to a barrister, or so the records hold. There were three other such Gate-houses in London: those of St. James's Palace, Lambeth Palace and St. John's Clerkenwell. Owing to 100

The old Gatehouse

years of philistine neglect this fine and splendid structure was unwillingly demolished in 1968. A trite pink replica pays shallow tribute to its predecessor. That a profession, which so strongly upholds tradition, should have conducted itself in this arbitrary manner deserves the Renaissance epitaph: 'Quod non fecerunt barbari fecerunt Barberini'—What the barbarians did not do, the Barberini (family) did.

At least the sturdy gates are preserved, carved in 1564.

STONE BUILDINGS

Sir Robert Taylor designed this classical building in 1775, a precursor to the complete redevelopment of the Inn. Fortunately the scheme proved too expensive and was abandoned. On the garden facade is a sun-dial placed there by William Pitt when he was Treasurer; see

Strand, built by James Gibb in 1714, and noted for one of its rectors, Thomas à Becket. Further West, a spiritual appetite is well satisfied by the secular premises of Simpson's Restaurant in the Strand, famed for its traditional English saddle of mutton trolley. The Savoy Hotel adjoins it, built with the profits of the Gilbert & Sullivan operettas, and is situated in the only street of London where you drive on the right. This enabled Mr. D'Oyly Carte's patrons to alight from their carriages at the entrance doors to the Savoy Theatre.

Opposite the Law Courts, note the 'Spy' cartoons in the window of the Wig & Pen Club. Nearby is Messrs. Twining's, the tea merchants who were responsible for the speedy tea-clipper trade to the Far East. At five and twenty past four of an afternoon, a worthy patron, Codrington Edmund Carrington by name, may be encountered (by asking the nice waitress Julia for your introduction to him). His ancestor was the great Chief Justice of Ceylon, the other tea isle, through whom England learnt to drink tea. He welcomes visitors from abroad and readers are recommended to make his acquaintance.

Closeby is to be found the Old Cheshire Cheese, a haven well worth the honour of Dr. Johnson's ghost. The delectable port-wine is most conducive to a full enjoyment of old England.

UP FLEET STREET

Cast your eyes across the roofs that lean over their street facades. This reveals their age more vividly than the shopfronts. The famous 'street of ink' has been associated with printing since 1500 (Caxton's assistant). The Solicitors' Law Stationery Society is where you buy a real writ for five pence. In close view are Coutts Bank (founded in 1692), bankers to Her Majesty the Queen, and Child's (established 1671), bankers to little Nell Gwynne.

The church of St. Dunstan's in the West gave its name to the Home for the Blind, and was mentioned by Dickens in 'The Chimes' of the lantern tower.

Backstage is Dr. Johnson's House (open to the public) at No. 17 Gough Square, where he compiled the great Dictionary. The learned Doctor died in Bolt Court hardby. Marvel at the newspaper superstructures that do so much to belittle the written word; and at the bottom of Fleet Street a stone marks the spot where young Edgar Wallace remained a street newsvendor, till he achieved world renown as a thriller writer.

Down the hill is St. Bride's (alias Bridget, and not of monogamous union), noted for the Roman excavations discovered there after the war. The Church is well associated with the lines of Richard Lovelace: 'Stone walls do not a prison make, nor iron bars a cage . . .'

the society. Realising the debt that posterity would acknowledge was theirs, the benchers invited the artist to dinner at which a golden cup filled with 500 gold sovereigns was placed discreetly before him.

Among the models for this grand opus were:

    Holman Hunt — Ina, King of Wessex
    Elma, Lady Lilford — Alfred the Great (Unisex)
    Lord Tennyson — Minos, King of Crete.

Unfortunately the fresco soon suffered the malady of the English climate that inflicts itself upon us all, but in 1890 it was successfully restored. This must have pleased the artist for he had earlier written: 'the faith I have in the justice of the time would console me, for the few who care to see my very best effort . . . I hear it is beginning to decay. I suppose it will go the way of all frescoes in England and speedily crumble away . . . Time is the only judge whose dictum is a serious matter to serious workers, but the destruction of one's work before it can receive judgment is a regret—even to the least vain'.

Perhaps this painting has inspired the post-war men of Lincoln's Inn: for the more active members of the Judiciary in office today are: the irrepressible Lord Chancellor, the ineffable Lord Chief Justice and the indispensable Master of the Rolls.

LINCOLN'S INN FIELDS

The largest square in London Town (twelve acres) was laid out by Inigo Jones in the seventeenth century. The towering plane trees shading the square well suit this green bonanza. For long it was a popular resort of duellists but to-day it is more noted for the minor speaker's corner (N.E.) to which aspiring advocates are sometimes known to acquire the common touch. Long before, as the name of Great Turnstile shows, the pathway through the Fields was a short-cut to the Strand from Holborn. In the years of Inigo Jones the square was the most fashionable in London. (Compare St. James's Square 1660 in the West End also one of the earliest squares in London). One plausible reason for its popularity was that Nell Gwynne resided here and her son, the Duke of St. Albans, was born in these lodgings.

The Royal College of Surgeons contains the museum of anatomy, and was designed by Sir Charles Barry in 1835. In the Large Room once was seen the skeleton of the Irish giant Byrne—all nine feet high. Alongside lay the infant Caroline Crachami who died at the age of ten, ten inches high. It is one of life's mysteries why the infant was not laid to rest in a Small Room.

The Old Curiosity Shop

Behind the Fields lies the 'Old' Curiosity Shop; a legacy of Charles Dickens' novel, so it is said. To the north, at No. 13, is Sir John Soane's Museum, set exactly as he left it at his death in 1837. A rare collection of antiquities are displayed in the rooms that he lived in and furnished.

A seat in memory of Margaret Macdonald, a resident, is to be seen in Canada Walk (north side) and is notable as one of the few London memorials to a woman other than a queen. Her husband, Ramsay Macdonald, was often host to other organisers of primeval socialism in the early years of this century. On one such occasion, guests of the first Labour Prime Minister were asked to leave their coats in the second bedroom. Before dinner was ended, the distressed housekeeper emerged and asked the company whether in future those who had coats would care to lay them on a bed not being slept in. The children had nearly suffocated. (Alas! This well illustrates Socialism: that worthy notions are oft rendered farcical by the inept conduct of their discharge).

Lincoln's Inn Fields Entrance

GRAY'S INN

INTRODUCTION

At Old Holborn, which connected Tyburn (the gallows at Marble Arch) to the Newgate Prison (now the Old Bailey) there reposes the Honourable Society of Gray's Inn. Its antecedents in history weave as old as the Temple itself. It started with the de Gray family on the site of whose manor the Inn is now situate. This 'certain Inn at Portepole' say the records in 1570, had gradually expanded to include the lawyers. The Paston Papers refer to a letter from the Chief Justice in 1484; a 'felaw' in Gray's Inn; while the Society's own books date back to 1569, the earlier records were burnt, and contain detailed records of the Honourable Society's activities, to wit a ledger accounts for the removal of a member's coat of arms at a cost of 8s 8d. The bearer was the Earl of Northumberland who had lent his name to an unsuccessful conspiracy against the crown.

In the reign of Henry VIII the Inn became so overcrowded that Sir Thomas Neville took the unprecedented step of accepting the Attorney-General as his bedfellow and in Ben Jonson's time the number of students doubled the collective number of the three other Inns.

The Inn's first heyday was during the reign of Queen Elizabeth I, when it became renowned for its spectacular revelries. The Queen was an enthusiastic visitor to the Inn, which to-day remembers her goodness in a toast: 'To the Pious, Glorious and Immortal memory of Good Queen Bess' on festive occasions. After her gracious presence, the Inn fell upon hard times, with fluctuating frequency, until the golden age of Dickens. The reason is simple: the role of lawyers is one of minding other people's business, and they often leave little time to look after their own. Wanton ruin befell the Inn in the last war, but through the tireless exertions of the post-war bench, the Inn's atmosphere is fully revived and the Inn does prosper happily.

The 'little' Inn is the mother of a famous family: Sir Francis Bacon; Sir Nicholas Bacon; Thomas Cromwell; Earl of Essex; Earl of Southampton; Sir Thomas Gresham (founder of the Royal Exchange); Lord Burghley; Sir Samuel Romilly; Sir Francis Walsingham; Sir Robert Lush; Hilaire Belloc; Sidney Webb; Lord Birkenhead; Lord Atkin; Sir Winston Churchill; Mr. Edward Heath, Prime Minister 1970; Mr. Selwyn Lloyd, incumbent Speaker of the House of Commons; Sir Robert Menzies, Prime Minister of Australia 1949–1966. Further linking 'the Revolting Colonies' was Joseph Ball, uncle to George Washington; and Franklin Roosevelt, President 1932–45.

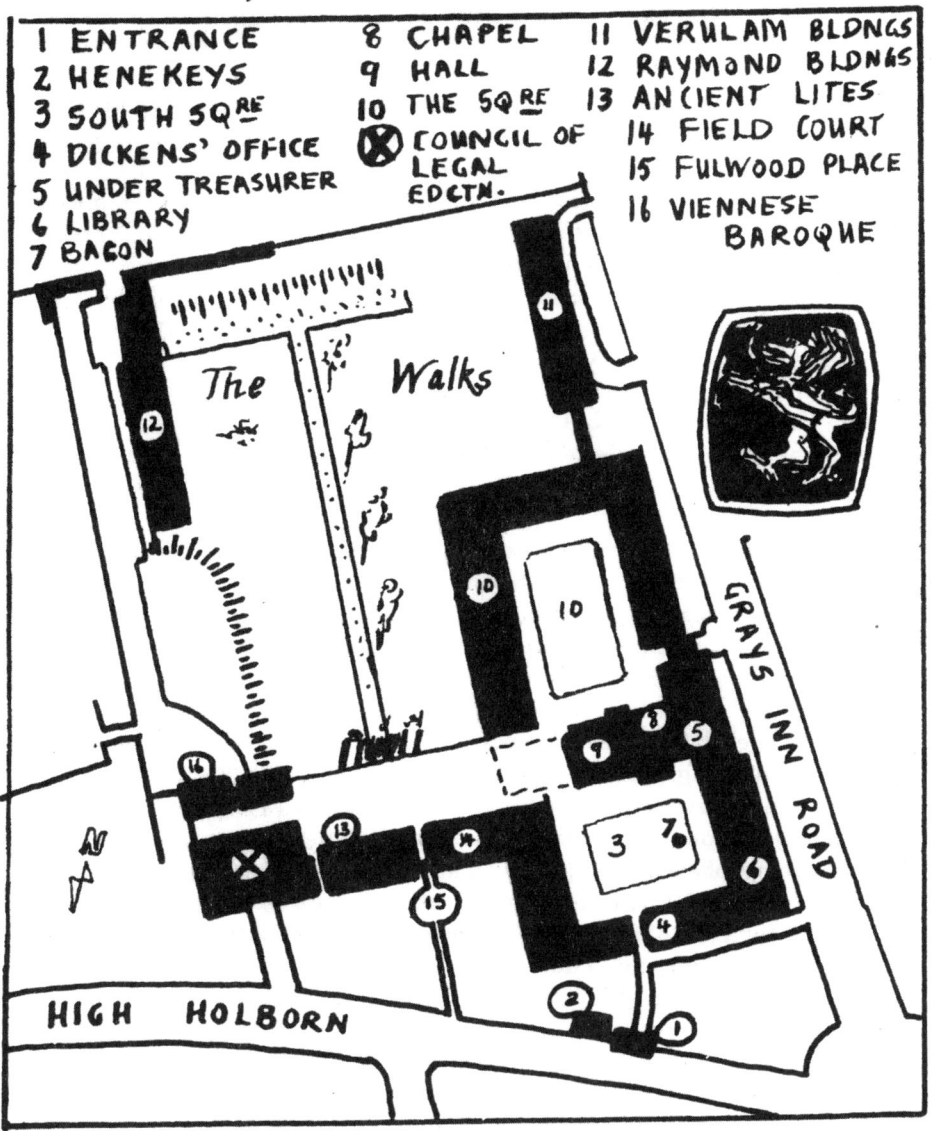

The Honourable Society of ~ GRAY'S INN

1 ENTRANCE
2 HENEKEYS
3 SOUTH SQ^{RE}
4 DICKENS' OFFICE
5 UNDER TREASURER
6 LIBRARY
7 BACON
8 CHAPEL
9 HALL
10 THE SQ^{RE}
ⓧ COUNCIL OF LEGAL EDCTN.
11 VERULAM BLDNGS
12 RAYMOND BLDNGS
13 ANCIENT LITES
14 FIELD COURT
15 FULWOOD PLACE
16 VIENNESE BAROQUE

THE GRIFFIN

The arms of Gray's Inn is a golden griffin 'segreant', on a black shield. This heraldic beast was employed by the ancients to guard golden treasure; its earliest decoration is believed to be in Persia

and at the Temple of Apollo, Miletus. A griffin is eight times larger than a lion (a fact not doubted, even by Albert Ramsbotham).

GRAY'S INN ENTRANCE

The seventeenth-century entrance from High Holborn is tucked aside Henekey's clock. Henekey's Wine Lodge is frequented by the younger members of Gray's Inn wherein is the old iron stove (1815) rescued from Gray's Inn Hall with the griffin motif by each grate. Old Holborn's Elizabethan Row (Staple Inn) merits the fact, en passant, as one of the few premises to survive the Great Fire. In the cellar of Maynards was secretly brewed the original recipe for the wine gum sweet.

    Passing through the archway, a '10 m.p.h. maximum' traffic sign obliges the pedestrian to observe the limit; for motorists are known not to be able to read. The fine figure of the Head Porter, Mr. J. R. McIntosh, commands the square that we enter:—

SOUTH SQUARE

Chains of offices link the Square, interposed by the pretty Hall (opposite). The statue by F. W. Pomeroy (who sculpted the Lady of Justice on the dome of the Old Bailey) laps the grass verge and is Sir Francis Bacon, the great Bacon, alias Shakespeare. Among his extraordinary gifts, he anticipated the twentieth century by 300 years when in a prelude to a masque performed by the society in 1594, he suggested: 'a zoo, a natural history museum, and in general a sky scraper' that leaves the drawing-board of Sir Basil Spence a pitcher beside a water-tower.

The nearside offices bring your eye to No. 1. Its mellowed brick explains the fact that it alone survived the last war. Here the teenager Charles Dickens, aged 15, was apprenticed in May 1827 to that hateful firm. As the reader is aware, the novelist-to-be soon moved down the lane to Fleet Street in November 1828 to exceed the 15s a week incoming as a clerk to the attorney Mr. Edward Blackmore. the Holker Library (framing the statue) was named after its donor who, dying without issue in 1882, left a bequest to his adopted child Gray's. Inspect the Geogian lead urns, troughs turned flower pots, before you reach—

GRAY'S INN HALL

The Hall was re-edified in the sixteenth century though it has been the focal point of the society's life for a much longerperiod. The aged brick (which survived the bombing) festoons the Inn with warm intimacy, unmatched by its counterparts. Although the roof was gutted by incendiaries in the war it and the Hall was faithfully restored through the generosity of the American Bar Association. A posse of benchers, it is said, handpicked the 200-year-old oaks for the above purpose.

Evelyn mentions the revels in the hall: 'which has relation neither to virtue nor policy'. The revels were last recorded in the year 1773 after which, the revellers emigrated to declare their independence in Boston. It is said that 'A Comedy of Errors' was first performed here on Holy Innocents' Day 1594. 'The Masque of Flowers' was regularly presented in the Hall though one Prynne had his ears cut off for abusing the Queen's love of the stage. It was at this time that Gray's assumed its lasting precedence over the other three Inns. The four Inns had squabbled as to the order of driving their carriages to Whitehall Palace to put on a masque. Gray's name was picked first out of the wig-box.

The fine screen which bolsters the near end of the hall was probably taken from a Spanish galleon in 1588. It survived the war because it was luckily removed from harm's way. Behind it is an old stone archway which was, so tradition has it, the entrance to Earl Gray's banqueting hall.

The plaques on the walls are original and depict the arms of each Treasurer. The large portraits hanging beside the windows are of famous legal figures, chief of whom is F. E. Smith, later Lord Chancellor Birkenhead.

The Parliament Clock was so termed when in the eighteenth century a tax was levied on every clock. This was evaded by placing clocks with large dials in taverns and other prominent public places.

Beneath the clock are more 'old Master' paintings: left to right: Sir Francis Bacon, L.C.; Sir Christopher Yelverton; Queen Elizabeth I; Lord Burghley; Sir Nicholas Bacon; Sir Francis Walsingham.

The north oriel window includes Gascoigne's coat of arms (Shakespeare's Lord Chief Justice in 'Henry IV') and the south oriel window was given by the American Bar Association. Across the dais is a bust of Sir Winston Churchill, an Honorary Bencher. It was in this hall that W.S.C. first met President Roosevelt.

Amongst this quality of historical festivity, the custom of 'Eating Dinners' is maintained. Before we leave the hall, the scene of great men's shadows through 600 years, shut your eyes and imagine a typical evening—the ponderous faces of the bench looking down upon the black-gowned rows of talkative aspirants. On any such evening a figure may rise from the lower floor. The hall echoes its conversation as the young man speaks out. Silence fills the flanks. All eyes turn upon him, waiting: he asks jocularly whether Benchers' Table have been given the same bill of fare as his own.

'Young fellow', commands the senior in the hall, 'your nostrils will lead you to the pinnacle of your profession, but your tongue will not.'

Being somewhat hungry, the young man answers: 'Sir Francis Bacon, would agree with you but his name did satisfy his appetite'...

THE CHAPEL

A place of worship has stood on the site of the present chapel since 1315. The court of Augmentations in 1539 investigated the duties of the chapel's priest (provided for by John le Grey in 1315). They held:

'that for tyme out of mynde' he had been required to 'synge & say masse for the studyent gentilmen & felaws of the house of Gray's Inn'.

The court of Augmentations was created by Henry VIII (29 CH. 27) to 'augment' or enlarge the revenues of the Crown up by the suppression of the monasteries; the Court long since became obsolete. Whether it is for this reason, or, perhaps, because of the onerous duty of saying the prayers daily that there is now no priest to preach the virtues of the departed, is a matter upon which posterity may speculate.

GRAY'S INN SQUARE

The entrance from Gray's Inn Road marks the site of the manor of Lord Gray. Consequently his chapel was built close by, where it stands to day although the outbuildings no longer surround it. The composition of the chapel garnished by the cupola, and the sedate buttressed hall anchored by the lantern tower, offset the perspective of the Georgian terraces. We may pay a compliment to the Master of the Walks for his skilful rendering of the flower-beds.

There once lived in the square a famous Political Baron, whose name could be seen on one doorway. In thirty years of public life, so it is said, he was unable to preserve his political allegiance . . . and he was known to his seniors as the 'penny-steamer' that 'plied from peer to peer'.

The hand-pump no longer works but marks the passageway to:

FIELD COURT

A cobbled thoroughfare leads to the portals of former town houses. 'Ancient Lites', the sign on the wall leading off Fulwood Place, is of legal interest. It warned its neighbours not to infringe the right of light that in time an owner acquires for his dwelling. Ironically, its present neighbour is the Council of Legal Education, a monstrous glasshouse which offends the quiet vicinity.

GRAYS INN WALKS

The imposing wrought-iron gates were made in 1723, when the Treasurer (T) was William (W) Gilbey (G). The gardens were laid

out by Bacon in his year of office as Treasurer, 1606, and the Catalpa trees can still be seen at the northern end of the Walks. Verulam Buildings were named after him, in 1803. The unlikely blue building to the west, with delicate balconies, is possibly the one example of Viennese Baroque in London.

This is the only spot known in London to enjoy the attention of the three great essayists—

'Still the best gardens in London'—Lamb.

'To touch on nature's tresses is my blessing'—Addison.

'Very well pleased with the sight of a fine lady walking', our tempting Pepys.

The gardens were once famed for the rookeries that had established themselves in the lofty plane trees but through the inadvertence of the society in 1875, the gardener was ordered to fell the trees without consideration for their nest-eggs. A Victorian ornithologist wrote: 'It is to be feared that the habitual users of the garden will soon hear with less sorrow when the same fate, as must happen in the natural course of events, over-takes the benchers! . . . So one barbarism engenders another'. Last year, it is surmised, a brace of duck took squatter's rights at nesting time. Before the Inn could appease its own conscience by offering residence, the duck flew back to Buckingham Palace whence they had strayed. A closer allegiance to their Queen, after all, is well worth living outside the Law.

~ URN IN ~
GRAYS INN SQUARE

LE FIN

Within these shadows sketched this guide takes leave:
The place of Dickens and the rest forget our hurried step . . .
If I awoke, Behold ! It was a dream; though yours, to peruse the morrow.

THE PUBLISHER'S POSTSCRIPT
ABOUT THE AUTHOR

T.D. was born in Mexico City in 1948, son of a diplomat. Has lived variously in Washington, Rome, New York, Helsinki, Cairo and Wellington. Great-nephew of an Inner Temple Bencher, he has found time to survey with a Cornish and cosmopolitan eye, the little-known by-ways of the profession he is about to enter.